50 Gourmet Mexican Dishes Recipes for Home

By: Kelly Johnson

Table of Contents

- Enchilada Suiza
- Mole Poblano
- Tacos al Pastor
- Chiles en Nogada
- Birria Tacos
- Tostadas de Ceviche
- Cochinita Pibil
- Camarones a la Diabla
- Pozole Verde
- Chilaquiles Rojos
- Molcajete
- Sopes
- Tamales de Elote
- Rajas con Crema
- Barbacoa de Res
- Pescado a la Veracruzana
- Guacamole with Pomegranate Seeds
- Tlayudas
- Tuna Tartare Tostadas
- Chile Rellenos
- Agua Fresca de Sandía
- Carnitas
- Salsa Verde Enchiladas
- Cactus Salad (Ensalada de Nopales)
- Birria Quesatacos
- Mole Oaxaqueño
- Huitlacoche Quesadillas
- Sopa de Lima
- Cochinita Pibil Tamales
- Pollo con Mole Amarillo
- Tacos Dorados
- Chile de Árbol Salsa
- Pulpo a la Gallega (Mexican-Spanish fusion)
- Pastel de Tres Leches
- Pambazos

- Nopales and Egg Tacos
- Chocolate Abuelita Pots de Crème
- Salsa Macha
- Tacos Gobernador
- Churros with Chocolate Dipping Sauce
- Carne Asada
- Huaraches
- Guava Paletas
- Poblano Cream Soup
- Chapulines Tostadas (grasshoppers)
- Mezcal-Infused Chocolate Truffles
- Queso Fundido with Chorizo
- Chile Ancho Rellenos de Picadillo
- Tequila-Lime Grilled Shrimp
- Jicama and Mango Salad

Enchilada Suiza

Ingredients:

For the Enchilada Sauce:

- 2 tablespoons vegetable oil
- 2 tablespoons all-purpose flour
- 3 tablespoons chili powder
- 1 teaspoon ground cumin
- 1/2 teaspoon garlic powder
- 1/4 teaspoon dried oregano
- 2 cups chicken or vegetable broth
- Salt to taste

For the Enchiladas:

- 8-10 corn tortillas
- 2 cups cooked and shredded chicken
- 1 cup sour cream
- 1 cup shredded Swiss cheese
- 1 cup shredded Monterey Jack cheese
- 1/2 cup chopped fresh cilantro
- Sliced green onions for garnish
- Avocado slices for serving

Instructions:

Enchilada Sauce:

In a saucepan, heat vegetable oil over medium heat.
Stir in flour, chili powder, cumin, garlic powder, and dried oregano. Cook for 1-2 minutes until fragrant.
Gradually whisk in chicken or vegetable broth, ensuring there are no lumps.
Simmer the sauce for 10-15 minutes, stirring occasionally, until it thickens.
Season with salt to taste.

Enchiladas:

Preheat the oven to 375°F (190°C).
In a mixing bowl, combine shredded chicken and 1/2 cup of the enchilada sauce. Set aside.
In a separate bowl, mix together sour cream, Swiss cheese, and Monterey Jack cheese.
Warm the corn tortillas in a dry skillet or microwave until pliable.
Spread a small amount of the cheese and sour cream mixture on each tortilla.
Spoon the chicken mixture onto each tortilla and roll them up, placing them seam-side down in a baking dish.
Pour the remaining enchilada sauce over the rolled tortillas.
Sprinkle the top with any remaining cheese mixture.
Bake in the preheated oven for 20-25 minutes or until the cheese is melted and bubbly.
Garnish with chopped cilantro, sliced green onions, and avocado slices.
Serve the Enchilada Suiza hot, and enjoy the deliciously cheesy and flavorful goodness!

Mole Poblano

Ingredients:

For the Mole Paste:

- 3 dried ancho chilies, stemmed and seeded
- 3 dried pasilla chilies, stemmed and seeded
- 2 dried mulato chilies, stemmed and seeded
- 2 tablespoons vegetable oil
- 1/2 cup almonds
- 1/4 cup sesame seeds
- 1/4 cup raisins
- 1/4 cup pumpkin seeds (pepitas)
- 3 cloves garlic, minced
- 1/2 cup chopped onions
- 1/2 teaspoon ground cinnamon
- 1/4 teaspoon ground cloves
- 1/4 teaspoon ground coriander
- 1/4 teaspoon ground cumin
- 1/4 teaspoon dried oregano
- 1/4 teaspoon ground black pepper
- 1/4 teaspoon ground anise seeds
- 1/4 teaspoon ground allspice
- 1/4 teaspoon ground thyme
- 2 tomatoes, roasted
- 1 corn tortilla, torn into pieces
- 1 stale bolillo or French roll, torn into pieces
- 3 cups chicken or vegetable broth
- Salt to taste

For the Mole Sauce:

- 2 tablespoons vegetable oil
- 1/2 cup dark chocolate, chopped
- 4 cups chicken or vegetable broth
- Salt to taste
- Sugar, if needed, to balance the flavors

For Serving:

- Cooked chicken, turkey, or other proteins
- Rice

Instructions:

Mole Paste:

> In a dry skillet over medium heat, toast the dried chilies until fragrant but not burnt. Remove and set aside.
> In the same skillet, heat 2 tablespoons of vegetable oil. Add almonds, sesame seeds, raisins, and pumpkin seeds. Toast until lightly browned.
> Add minced garlic and chopped onions. Sauté until onions are translucent.
> Add the toasted chilies, ground spices, roasted tomatoes, torn tortilla, and torn bolillo or French roll to the skillet. Mix well.
> Pour in 3 cups of chicken or vegetable broth. Simmer for about 15-20 minutes until the ingredients are soft.
> Allow the mixture to cool slightly and then blend until smooth. Add more broth if needed.

Mole Sauce:

> In a large pot, heat 2 tablespoons of vegetable oil over medium heat.
> Add the blended mole paste to the pot. Cook for 5-7 minutes, stirring constantly.
> Add the chopped dark chocolate and continue stirring until the chocolate is melted.
> Gradually add 4 cups of chicken or vegetable broth, stirring constantly to avoid lumps.
> Season with salt and adjust the sweetness with sugar if needed.
> Simmer the mole sauce for 30-40 minutes until it thickens.

To Serve:

> Serve the Mole Poblano over cooked chicken, turkey, or other proteins.
> Optionally, serve with rice on the side.
> Enjoy the rich and complex flavors of this traditional Mexican mole!

Tacos al Pastor

Ingredients:

For the Marinade:

- 3 dried guajillo chilies, stemmed and seeded
- 2 dried ancho chilies, stemmed and seeded
- 3 cloves garlic
- 1/2 small onion, roughly chopped
- 1/4 cup pineapple juice
- 2 tablespoons white vinegar
- 1 teaspoon dried oregano
- 1 teaspoon ground cumin
- 1 teaspoon smoked paprika
- 1/2 teaspoon ground cinnamon
- Salt and black pepper to taste

For the Tacos:

- 2 pounds pork shoulder, thinly sliced
- 1/2 pineapple, peeled, cored, and sliced into thin rounds
- Corn tortillas
- Fresh cilantro, chopped, for garnish
- Diced onion, for garnish
- Sliced radishes, for garnish
- Lime wedges, for serving

Instructions:

Marinade:

In a dry skillet over medium heat, toast the dried guajillo and ancho chilies for 1-2 minutes until fragrant. Remove from heat.
In a blender, combine the toasted chilies, garlic, onion, pineapple juice, white vinegar, oregano, cumin, smoked paprika, cinnamon, salt, and black pepper. Blend until you have a smooth paste.

Place the sliced pork in a large bowl and coat it with the marinade. Cover and refrigerate for at least 4 hours or overnight.

Tacos:

Preheat your grill or grill pan over medium-high heat.
Thread the marinated pork slices onto skewers, alternating with pineapple slices.
Grill the skewers for 15-20 minutes, turning occasionally, until the pork is cooked through and slightly charred.
Warm the corn tortillas on the grill for about 20 seconds on each side.
Remove the pork and pineapple from the skewers.
Assemble the tacos by placing a few slices of grilled pork and pineapple on each tortilla.
Garnish with chopped cilantro, diced onion, and sliced radishes.
Serve the Tacos al Pastor hot with lime wedges on the side.
Enjoy the delicious and authentic flavors of Tacos al Pastor!

Chiles en Nogada

Ingredients:

For the Filling:

- 6 large poblano peppers, roasted, peeled, and seeds removed
- 1 pound ground pork or beef
- 1/2 cup onion, finely chopped
- 2 cloves garlic, minced
- 1/2 cup tomatoes, diced
- 1/4 cup raisins
- 1/4 cup almonds, chopped
- 1/4 cup candied pineapple, diced
- 1/4 cup peach or pear, diced
- 1/2 teaspoon ground cinnamon
- 1/4 teaspoon ground cloves
- Salt and black pepper to taste
- 2 tablespoons vegetable oil

For the Nogada Sauce:

- 1 cup walnuts, shelled and peeled
- 1 cup queso fresco or cream cheese
- 1 cup milk
- 1/4 cup sugar
- 1/4 teaspoon ground cinnamon
- Salt to taste

For Garnish:

- Pomegranate seeds
- Fresh parsley, chopped

Instructions:

Filling:

> In a large skillet, heat vegetable oil over medium heat.
> Add chopped onion and garlic, sauté until translucent.

Add ground pork or beef, cooking until browned.
Stir in diced tomatoes, raisins, chopped almonds, candied pineapple, peach or pear, ground cinnamon, ground cloves, salt, and black pepper.
Cook the filling for about 10-15 minutes until the flavors meld together. Set aside.

Nogada Sauce:

In a blender, combine shelled and peeled walnuts, queso fresco or cream cheese, milk, sugar, ground cinnamon, and salt.
Blend until you achieve a smooth, creamy consistency. Adjust sugar and salt to taste.

Assembly:

Stuff each roasted poblano pepper with the filling mixture.
Cover the stuffed peppers with the nogada sauce.
Garnish with pomegranate seeds and chopped fresh parsley.
Serve Chiles en Nogada at room temperature or slightly chilled.
Enjoy this traditional Mexican dish that combines savory and sweet flavors in a delightful way!

Birria Tacos

Ingredients:

For the Birria:

- 3 pounds beef chuck roast or goat meat, cut into chunks
- 5 dried guajillo chilies, stemmed and seeded
- 3 dried ancho chilies, stemmed and seeded
- 4 cloves garlic, minced
- 1 medium onion, chopped
- 1 teaspoon dried oregano
- 1 teaspoon ground cumin
- 1 teaspoon smoked paprika
- 1/2 teaspoon ground cinnamon
- Salt and black pepper to taste
- 3 bay leaves
- 4 cups beef or vegetable broth
- 1/4 cup apple cider vinegar
- 1 tablespoon vegetable oil

For Assembling Tacos:

- Corn tortillas
- Diced onions and fresh cilantro for garnish
- Lime wedges for serving

Instructions:

Birria:

Preheat the oven to 350°F (175°C).
In a dry skillet over medium heat, toast the dried guajillo and ancho chilies for about 1-2 minutes until fragrant. Remove from heat.
In a blender, combine the toasted chilies, minced garlic, chopped onion, dried oregano, ground cumin, smoked paprika, ground cinnamon, salt, and black pepper. Add a bit of water if needed to blend into a smooth paste.

In a large pot or Dutch oven, heat vegetable oil over medium-high heat. Sear the meat chunks until browned on all sides.

Add the chili paste to the pot and cook for 2-3 minutes, stirring constantly.

Pour in the beef or vegetable broth, apple cider vinegar, and add bay leaves. Stir well.

Cover the pot and transfer it to the preheated oven. Cook for about 2.5 to 3 hours or until the meat is tender and easily shreds.

Remove from the oven and shred the meat using two forks.

Assembling Tacos:

Heat corn tortillas on a griddle or skillet until warm and pliable.

Spoon the birria meat onto each tortilla.

Garnish with diced onions, fresh cilantro, and a squeeze of lime juice.

Optionally, serve with a cup of the birria broth for dipping.

Serve the Birria Tacos hot and enjoy the rich and flavorful goodness!

Note: Birria tacos are often served with a side of consommé (the cooking broth) for dipping, providing an extra layer of flavor.

Tostadas de Ceviche

Ingredients:

For the Ceviche:

- 1 pound white fish fillets (tilapia, snapper, or halibut), diced into small pieces
- 1 cup cherry tomatoes, halved
- 1 cucumber, peeled and diced
- 1/2 red onion, finely chopped
- 1 jalapeño, seeds removed and finely chopped
- 1/2 cup fresh cilantro, chopped
- Juice of 4-5 limes
- Juice of 1 orange
- Salt and black pepper to taste
- Avocado slices for garnish

For the Tostadas:

- Corn tostadas
- Avocado slices
- Radishes, thinly sliced
- Fresh cilantro, chopped
- Lime wedges for serving

Instructions:

Ceviche:

In a large bowl, combine diced fish, cherry tomatoes, cucumber, red onion, jalapeño, and fresh cilantro.
Squeeze the juice of limes and orange over the mixture.
Season with salt and black pepper to taste.
Gently toss the ingredients until the fish is evenly coated with the citrus juices.
Cover the bowl with plastic wrap and refrigerate for at least 30 minutes to allow the fish to "cook" in the citrus juices.

Tostadas:

Arrange corn tostadas on a serving platter.

Spoon the ceviche mixture onto each tostada.
Top each tostada with avocado slices, thinly sliced radishes, and chopped fresh cilantro.
Serve Tostadas de Ceviche with lime wedges on the side.
Enjoy these refreshing and flavorful tostadas as a delightful appetizer or light meal!

Cochinita Pibil

Ingredients:

For the Achiote Marinade:

- 3 tablespoons achiote (annatto) paste
- 3 tablespoons orange juice
- 2 tablespoons white vinegar
- 2 tablespoons lime juice
- 3 cloves garlic, minced
- 1 teaspoon ground cumin
- 1 teaspoon dried oregano
- 1/2 teaspoon ground cinnamon
- Salt and black pepper to taste

For the Cochinita Pibil:

- 3 pounds pork shoulder, cut into chunks
- Banana leaves (for wrapping, optional)
- 1 red onion, thinly sliced
- 2 oranges, sliced
- Corn tortillas for serving
- Pickled red onions for garnish (optional)

Instructions:

Achiote Marinade:

In a blender, combine achiote paste, orange juice, white vinegar, lime juice, minced garlic, ground cumin, dried oregano, ground cinnamon, salt, and black pepper.
Blend until you have a smooth, vibrant orange marinade.

Cochinita Pibil:

Place the pork chunks in a large bowl and coat them with the achiote marinade. Ensure each piece is well covered. Cover the bowl and marinate in the refrigerator for at least 4 hours or overnight.
Preheat the oven to 325°F (163°C).

If using banana leaves, briefly pass them over an open flame to soften and make them more pliable.

Line a baking dish with banana leaves or parchment paper.

Place the marinated pork in the dish and top it with sliced red onions and oranges.

Wrap the pork in the banana leaves or cover it tightly with parchment paper, then cover the dish with aluminum foil.

Bake in the preheated oven for 3 to 4 hours or until the pork is tender and easily shreds.

Serve the Cochinita Pibil on corn tortillas, garnished with pickled red onions if desired.

Enjoy this traditional Yucatán dish with its rich flavors and tender, slow-cooked pork!

Camarones a la Diabla

Ingredients:

- 1 pound large shrimp, peeled and deveined
- 4 dried guajillo chilies, stemmed and seeded
- 3 dried arbol chilies, stemmed and seeded
- 3 cloves garlic, minced
- 1/2 cup tomato puree
- 1/4 cup chicken or shrimp broth
- 2 tablespoons vegetable oil
- 1 onion, finely chopped
- 1 teaspoon dried oregano
- 1 teaspoon ground cumin
- Salt and black pepper to taste
- Lime wedges for serving
- Chopped fresh cilantro for garnish

Instructions:

In a dry skillet over medium heat, toast the dried guajillo and arbol chilies for about 1-2 minutes until fragrant. Remove from heat.
In a bowl, cover the toasted chilies with hot water and let them soak for 15-20 minutes until softened.
Drain the chilies and transfer them to a blender. Add minced garlic, tomato puree, and chicken or shrimp broth. Blend until you have a smooth sauce.
Heat vegetable oil in a large skillet over medium heat. Add finely chopped onions and cook until they become translucent.
Pour the chili sauce from the blender into the skillet. Stir in dried oregano, ground cumin, salt, and black pepper. Simmer for 10-15 minutes to allow the flavors to meld.
Add the peeled and deveined shrimp to the skillet, ensuring they are well-coated with the sauce. Cook for 5-7 minutes or until the shrimp are pink and cooked through.
Adjust seasoning if needed.
Serve Camarones a la Diabla hot, garnished with chopped fresh cilantro and lime wedges on the side.
Enjoy these spicy and flavorful shrimp with a touch of heat!

Pozole Verde

Ingredients:

For the Pozole:

- 2 pounds boneless, skinless chicken thighs
- 2 cans (29 ounces each) hominy, drained and rinsed
- 1 onion, quartered
- 4 cloves garlic, minced
- 1 teaspoon dried oregano
- 8 cups chicken broth
- Salt to taste

For the Green Sauce:

- 4 cups fresh tomatillos, husked and rinsed
- 2-3 jalapeños, seeds removed (adjust to taste)
- 1 cup fresh cilantro leaves
- 1 onion, coarsely chopped
- 4 cloves garlic
- 1 teaspoon ground cumin
- Salt to taste

For Garnish:

- Shredded cabbage
- Radishes, sliced
- Avocado, sliced
- Fresh cilantro, chopped
- Lime wedges
- Tortilla chips or tostadas

Instructions:

Pozole:

In a large pot, combine chicken thighs, hominy, quartered onion, minced garlic, dried oregano, and chicken broth.

Bring the mixture to a boil, then reduce the heat to low. Simmer for 1 to 1.5 hours or until the chicken is tender and easily shreds.

Remove the chicken thighs from the pot, shred the meat, and return it to the pot. Season the pozole with salt to taste.

Green Sauce:

In a blender, combine tomatillos, jalapeños, cilantro leaves, coarsely chopped onion, minced garlic, ground cumin, and salt.

Blend until you have a smooth green sauce.

Pour the green sauce into the pot with the pozole, stirring to combine. Simmer for an additional 15-20 minutes.

To Serve:

Ladle the Pozole Verde into bowls.

Garnish with shredded cabbage, sliced radishes, avocado slices, chopped fresh cilantro, and lime wedges.

Serve with tortilla chips or tostadas on the side.

Enjoy this delicious and comforting Pozole Verde, a traditional Mexican soup with a flavorful green twist!

Chilaquiles Rojos

Ingredients:

For the Red Sauce:

- 4 large tomatoes, chopped
- 2-3 dried guajillo chilies, stemmed and seeded
- 2-3 dried arbol chilies, stemmed and seeded
- 1/2 onion, chopped
- 2 cloves garlic, minced
- 1 teaspoon dried oregano
- 1/2 teaspoon ground cumin
- 2 cups chicken or vegetable broth
- Salt to taste

For the Chilaquiles:

- 10-12 corn tortillas, cut into triangles
- Vegetable oil for frying
- 2 cups shredded cooked chicken (optional)
- 1 cup crumbled queso fresco or feta cheese
- 1/2 cup sour cream
- Sliced red onions for garnish
- Chopped fresh cilantro for garnish
- Avocado slices for serving
- Lime wedges for serving

Instructions:

Red Sauce:

> In a dry skillet over medium heat, toast the dried guajillo and arbol chilies for about 1-2 minutes until fragrant. Remove from heat.
> In a blender, combine the toasted chilies, chopped tomatoes, chopped onion, minced garlic, dried oregano, ground cumin, and chicken or vegetable broth. Blend until smooth.

Strain the sauce through a fine mesh sieve into a bowl, pressing down to extract as much liquid as possible. Discard the solids.
Pour the strained sauce back into the blender and blend again until smooth. Season with salt to taste.

Chilaquiles:

In a large skillet, heat vegetable oil over medium-high heat.
Fry the tortilla triangles in batches until golden and crispy. Remove and place them on paper towels to drain excess oil.
In the same skillet, pour the red sauce and bring it to a simmer. Add the fried tortilla triangles and toss until they are well-coated with the sauce.
If using, add shredded cooked chicken to the skillet and toss until heated through.
Transfer the Chilaquiles Rojos to a serving platter.
Garnish with crumbled queso fresco or feta cheese, dollops of sour cream, sliced red onions, and chopped fresh cilantro.
Serve with avocado slices and lime wedges on the side.
Enjoy these delicious Chilaquiles Rojos for breakfast or brunch, or anytime you crave a flavorful and comforting dish!

Molcajete

Ingredients:

For the Salsa:

- 4 large tomatoes, diced
- 1/2 onion, finely chopped
- 2-3 jalapeños, finely chopped (adjust to taste)
- 2 cloves garlic, minced
- 1/4 cup fresh cilantro, chopped
- Juice of 2 limes
- Salt and black pepper to taste

For the Guacamole:

- 3 ripe avocados, mashed
- 1/4 cup red onion, finely chopped
- 1/4 cup fresh cilantro, chopped
- 1 jalapeño, seeds removed and finely chopped
- Juice of 1 lime
- Salt to taste

For the Refried Beans:

- 1 can (15 ounces) pinto or black beans, drained and rinsed
- 2 tablespoons vegetable oil
- 1/2 onion, finely chopped
- 2 cloves garlic, minced
- 1 teaspoon ground cumin
- Salt and black pepper to taste

For the Grilled Meats:

- 1 pound skirt steak, thinly sliced
- 1 pound chicken breasts, thinly sliced
- 1 pound large shrimp, peeled and deveined

- Juice of 2 limes
- 1 teaspoon chili powder
- Salt and black pepper to taste
- Vegetable oil for grilling

Other Ingredients:

- Queso fresco, crumbled
- Tortillas for serving

Instructions:

Salsa:

In a molcajete, combine diced tomatoes, finely chopped onion, jalapeños, minced garlic, chopped cilantro, lime juice, salt, and black pepper.
Use the pestle to crush and mix the ingredients until you have a chunky salsa.

Guacamole:

In another section of the molcajete, combine mashed avocados, finely chopped red onion, chopped cilantro, finely chopped jalapeño, lime juice, and salt.
Crush and mix until you achieve a creamy guacamole consistency.

Refried Beans:

In a small skillet, heat vegetable oil over medium heat. Add finely chopped onion and minced garlic, cooking until softened.
Add drained and rinsed beans, ground cumin, salt, and black pepper. Mash the beans with a fork or potato masher, creating a coarse consistency.

Grilled Meats:

In a bowl, marinate sliced skirt steak, chicken breasts, and shrimp with lime juice, chili powder, salt, and black pepper.
Heat a grill or grill pan over medium-high heat. Grill the marinated meats until cooked through and slightly charred.

Assembly:

In the molcajete, arrange the salsa, guacamole, refried beans, grilled meats, and crumbled queso fresco in sections.

Serve the Molcajete Mixto with warm tortillas on the side.

Each diner can create their own tacos or enjoy the flavorful mixture directly from the molcajete.

Enjoy this festive and communal dish, perfect for sharing with friends and family!

Sopes

Ingredients:

For the Sopes:

- 2 cups masa harina (corn flour)
- 1 1/4 cups warm water
- 1/2 teaspoon salt
- 1 cup refried beans
- 1 cup cooked and shredded chicken or beef (seasoned to taste)
- 1 cup lettuce, shredded
- 1 cup queso fresco or Mexican cheese, crumbled
- 1 cup salsa (red or green)
- Vegetable oil for frying

Optional Toppings:

- Chopped tomatoes
- Sliced radishes
- Sour cream
- Avocado slices
- Fresh cilantro, chopped

Instructions:

Sopes Dough:

In a large bowl, combine masa harina, warm water, and salt. Mix until you have a smooth dough.
Divide the dough into golf ball-sized portions.
Flatten each ball into a disk, creating a small well in the center with your thumb.
Heat vegetable oil in a skillet over medium heat.
Fry each sope in the hot oil until golden brown and cooked through, around 2-3 minutes per side.
Drain excess oil on paper towels.

Assembling Sopes:

Spread a layer of refried beans onto each fried sope.

Add a portion of cooked and shredded chicken or beef on top of the beans.
Sprinkle shredded lettuce over the meat.
Drizzle with salsa and sprinkle crumbled queso fresco or Mexican cheese on top.

Optional Toppings:

Garnish with chopped tomatoes, sliced radishes, dollops of sour cream, avocado slices, and fresh cilantro.
Serve immediately, allowing each person to customize their sopes with their favorite toppings.
Enjoy these delicious and versatile sopes as a delightful appetizer or a satisfying main dish!

Tamales de Elote

Ingredients:

For the Tamale Dough:

- 4 cups fresh corn kernels (about 6-8 ears of corn)
- 1 cup cornmeal
- 1 cup unsalted butter, softened
- 1 cup granulated sugar
- 1 teaspoon baking powder
- 1/2 teaspoon salt
- 1 cup milk
- Corn husks, soaked in warm water for at least 30 minutes

For Filling (Optional):

- Sweetened condensed milk
- Cinnamon sugar

Instructions:

Preparing the Corn:

Using a knife, carefully remove the corn kernels from the cobs.
In a blender, blend 2 cups of the corn kernels until smooth. Keep the remaining 2 cups of corn kernels whole.

Tamale Dough:

In a large mixing bowl, beat the softened butter and sugar together until light and fluffy.
Add the blended corn, cornmeal, baking powder, and salt to the butter-sugar mixture. Mix well.
Gradually add milk while continuing to mix until you have a smooth, creamy batter.
Fold in the whole corn kernels into the batter, ensuring they are evenly distributed.

Assembling Tamales:

Take a corn husk and spread a thin layer of the tamale dough on the center, leaving some space at the edges.

If desired, add a spoonful of sweetened condensed milk or sprinkle with cinnamon sugar in the center of the dough.

Fold the sides of the corn husk over the dough, creating a cylindrical shape.

Fold the bottom of the husk up and secure it with kitchen twine or a thin strip of corn husk.

Steaming Tamales:

Arrange the tamales in a steamer, standing them upright with the folded end at the bottom.

Steam the tamales for approximately 1 to 1.5 hours or until the dough is firm.

Allow the tamales to cool slightly before serving.

Serve Tamales de Elote warm and enjoy this delicious sweet corn treat!

These tamales can be enjoyed on their own or with a side of Mexican hot chocolate.

Rajas con Crema

Ingredients:

- 4 poblano peppers, roasted, peeled, seeded, and sliced into strips
- 1 large onion, thinly sliced
- 2 tablespoons vegetable oil
- 2 cloves garlic, minced
- 1 cup Mexican crema or sour cream
- 1 cup Oaxaca cheese or Monterrey Jack cheese, shredded
- Salt and black pepper to taste
- Fresh cilantro, chopped, for garnish
- Warm tortillas for serving

Instructions:

Roast and Prep Poblano Peppers:
- Roast poblano peppers over an open flame or under the broiler until the skin is charred.
- Place the roasted peppers in a plastic bag for a few minutes to steam, making it easier to peel the skin.
- Peel, seed, and slice the poblano peppers into thin strips.

Sauté Onion and Garlic:
- In a large skillet, heat vegetable oil over medium heat.
- Add thinly sliced onions and sauté until softened and translucent.
- Add minced garlic and sauté for an additional 1-2 minutes until fragrant.

Add Poblano Strips:
- Add the sliced poblano peppers to the skillet with the onions and garlic. Stir to combine.

Creamy Sauce:
- Pour Mexican crema or sour cream over the poblano mixture. Stir well to coat the peppers evenly.

Cheese and Seasoning:
- Sprinkle shredded Oaxaca or Monterrey Jack cheese over the mixture.
- Season with salt and black pepper to taste.

Simmer:
- Reduce the heat to low and let the mixture simmer until the cheese melts and the flavors meld, about 5-7 minutes.

Garnish and Serve:
- Garnish with chopped fresh cilantro.
- Serve the Rajas con Crema warm with warm tortillas on the side.

Enjoy:
- Serve this delicious Rajas con Crema as a side dish or as a filling for tacos or quesadillas.

This dish combines the mild heat of poblano peppers with the creamy richness of Mexican crema and cheese, creating a flavorful and satisfying dish.

Barbacoa de Res

Ingredients:

For the Barbacoa:

- 3 pounds beef cheek meat or beef chuck roast, cut into large chunks
- 1 large onion, chopped
- 4 cloves garlic, minced
- 2 bay leaves
- 1 tablespoon ground cumin
- 1 tablespoon dried oregano
- 1 teaspoon smoked paprika
- 1 teaspoon ground cloves
- 1 teaspoon ground cinnamon
- 1 chipotle pepper in adobo sauce, chopped (optional for extra heat)
- Salt and black pepper to taste
- 1 cup beef broth
- Juice of 2 limes
- 1/4 cup apple cider vinegar

For Serving:

- Corn tortillas
- Chopped fresh cilantro
- Diced onions
- Lime wedges
- Salsa or hot sauce

Instructions:

Prepare the Meat:
- Trim excess fat from the beef cheek meat or chuck roast and cut it into large chunks.

Seasoning Mix:
- In a bowl, combine chopped onion, minced garlic, bay leaves, ground cumin, dried oregano, smoked paprika, ground cloves, ground cinnamon, chopped chipotle pepper (if using), salt, and black pepper.

Marinate the Meat:

- Rub the beef chunks with the seasoning mix, ensuring each piece is well-coated.
- Let the meat marinate for at least 30 minutes or refrigerate overnight for enhanced flavor.

Cooking the Barbacoa:
- In a large pot or slow cooker, place the marinated beef chunks.
- Pour beef broth, lime juice, and apple cider vinegar over the meat.
- Cover and cook on low heat for 6-8 hours in a slow cooker or on the stovetop until the beef is tender and easily shreds.

Shred the Meat:
- Once cooked, shred the beef using two forks. It should be tender and moist.

Serve:
- Warm corn tortillas and spoon the shredded beef onto them.
- Top with chopped fresh cilantro, diced onions, and a squeeze of lime juice.
- Serve with your favorite salsa or hot sauce on the side.

Enjoy:
- Enjoy the Barbacoa de Res tacos, traditionally served with flavorful and aromatic beef that's been slow-cooked to perfection.

This Barbacoa de Res is perfect for tacos, burritos, or served with rice and beans for a hearty meal.

Pescado a la Veracruzana

Ingredients:

- 4 white fish fillets (such as snapper or grouper), about 6 ounces each
- Salt and black pepper to taste
- 2 tablespoons olive oil
- 1 onion, thinly sliced
- 2 bell peppers (preferably red and green), thinly sliced
- 3 cloves garlic, minced
- 2 cups tomatoes, diced
- 1/2 cup green olives, sliced
- 2 tablespoons capers, drained
- 3 bay leaves
- 1 teaspoon dried oregano
- 1/2 teaspoon dried thyme
- 1/2 cup white wine or chicken broth
- Juice of 1 lime
- Fresh cilantro or parsley for garnish

Instructions:

Season and Sear the Fish:
- Season the fish fillets with salt and black pepper.
- In a large skillet, heat olive oil over medium-high heat. Sear the fish fillets for 2-3 minutes on each side or until golden. Remove from the skillet and set aside.

Sauté Vegetables:
- In the same skillet, add sliced onions and bell peppers. Sauté until softened.

Add Aromatics:
- Stir in minced garlic and cook for an additional minute until fragrant.

Create Tomato Sauce:
- Add diced tomatoes, green olives, capers, bay leaves, dried oregano, and dried thyme to the skillet. Stir to combine.

Simmer with Wine or Broth:
- Pour in white wine or chicken broth to deglaze the skillet, scraping any browned bits from the bottom.

Cook Fish in Sauce:
- Return the seared fish fillets to the skillet, nestling them into the tomato mixture.
- Cover the skillet and simmer for 8-10 minutes or until the fish is cooked through.

Finish and Garnish:
- Drizzle lime juice over the fish.
- Garnish with fresh cilantro or parsley.

Serve:
- Serve the Pescado a la Veracruzana over rice or with crusty bread to soak up the flavorful tomato sauce.

Enjoy:
- Enjoy this delightful Veracruz-style fish dish with its vibrant flavors and a perfect blend of savory and tangy elements.

Guacamole with Pomegranate Seeds

Ingredients:

- 3 ripe avocados, peeled, pitted, and mashed
- 1 small red onion, finely diced
- 1-2 jalapeños, seeds and membranes removed, finely minced
- 1-2 cloves garlic, minced
- 1-2 tomatoes, diced
- Juice of 2 limes
- Salt and black pepper to taste
- 1/2 cup fresh cilantro, chopped
- 1/2 cup pomegranate seeds (arils)

Instructions:

Prepare the Avocados:
- Cut the avocados in half, remove the pits, and scoop the flesh into a bowl.

Mash the Avocados:
- Mash the avocados with a fork or potato masher until you achieve your desired consistency.

Add Aromatics:
- Add finely diced red onion, minced jalapeños, and minced garlic to the mashed avocados.

Incorporate Tomatoes:
- Gently fold in the diced tomatoes, ensuring even distribution.

Season:
- Squeeze the juice of two limes into the guacamole.
- Season with salt and black pepper to taste. Adjust the seasoning as needed.

Add Fresh Cilantro:
- Stir in the chopped fresh cilantro for a burst of flavor.

Fold in Pomegranate Seeds:
- Carefully fold in the pomegranate seeds (arils) into the guacamole.

Chill (Optional):
- If time allows, cover the guacamole and refrigerate for about 30 minutes to let the flavors meld.

Serve:

- Serve the Guacamole with Pomegranate Seeds with tortilla chips or as a topping for tacos, nachos, or grilled meats.

Enjoy:
- Enjoy the delightful combination of creamy guacamole with the sweet and juicy burst of pomegranate seeds, adding a unique twist to this classic dip!

Tlayudas

Ingredients:

For the Tlayudas:

- 4 large corn tortillas
- 1 cup refried black beans
- 2 cups Oaxaca cheese or Monterey Jack cheese, shredded
- 1 cup shredded lettuce
- 1 cup thinly sliced radishes
- 1 cup avocado slices
- 1 cup salsa (red or green)
- 1/2 cup crumbled queso fresco or feta cheese
- 1/4 cup fresh cilantro, chopped
- Lime wedges for serving

Optional Protein Additions:

- Grilled chicken, beef, or chorizo

Instructions:

Prepare the Tortillas:
- Preheat a comal, griddle, or large skillet over medium-high heat.
- Lightly toast the corn tortillas on both sides until they become crispy but still pliable.

Spread Refried Beans:
- Spread a layer of refried black beans evenly over each tortilla, leaving a border around the edges.

Add Cheese:
- Sprinkle a generous amount of shredded Oaxaca or Monterey Jack cheese over the beans, covering the entire surface.

Optional Protein (if using):
- If you're adding grilled chicken, beef, or chorizo, place the cooked protein on top of the cheese.

Heat Tlayudas:

- Place the tlayudas on the preheated comal or skillet and cook until the cheese is melted, and the tortillas are crispy at the edges.

Finish Assembling:
- Remove the tlayudas from the heat and add shredded lettuce, sliced radishes, avocado slices, crumbled queso fresco or feta cheese, and chopped fresh cilantro.

Drizzle with Salsa:
- Drizzle salsa (red or green) over the toppings, according to your preference.

Serve:
- Serve the tlayudas immediately while they are warm and crispy.

Garnish:
- Garnish with lime wedges on the side for squeezing over the tlayudas.

Enjoy:
- Enjoy the delicious flavors and textures of tlayudas, a traditional Oaxacan street food, with a variety of fresh toppings and optional protein.

Tuna Tartare Tostadas

Ingredients:

For the Tuna Tartare:

- 1/2 pound sushi-grade tuna, finely diced
- 2 tablespoons soy sauce
- 1 tablespoon sesame oil
- 1 tablespoon rice vinegar
- 1 teaspoon honey
- 1 teaspoon fresh ginger, grated
- 1 teaspoon sesame seeds
- 1 green onion, finely chopped
- Salt and pepper to taste

For the Tostadas:

- 8 small corn tostadas
- 1 avocado, thinly sliced
- 1 radish, thinly sliced
- Fresh cilantro leaves for garnish
- Lime wedges for serving

Instructions:

Prepare Tuna Tartare:
- In a bowl, combine diced tuna, soy sauce, sesame oil, rice vinegar, honey, grated ginger, sesame seeds, and chopped green onion.
- Season with salt and pepper to taste. Mix gently to combine.
- Refrigerate the tuna tartare for about 15-20 minutes to allow the flavors to meld.

Assemble Tostadas:
- Place a spoonful of tuna tartare on each corn tostada.

Add Avocado and Radish:
- Top each tostada with a few slices of avocado and radish.

Garnish:

- Garnish with fresh cilantro leaves.

Serve with Lime Wedges:
- Serve the tuna tartare tostadas with lime wedges on the side for squeezing over the top.

Enjoy:
- Enjoy these refreshing and flavorful tuna tartare tostadas as a light and elegant appetizer or snack.

Note: Ensure that the tuna used is labeled as sushi-grade or suitable for raw consumption to ensure safety.

Chile Rellenos

Ingredients:

For the Chiles Rellenos:

- 4 large poblano peppers
- 1 cup queso fresco or Oaxaca cheese, shredded
- 4 large eggs, separated
- 1/2 cup all-purpose flour
- Salt and pepper to taste
- Vegetable oil for frying

For the Tomato Sauce:

- 4 large tomatoes, chopped
- 1/2 onion, chopped
- 2 cloves garlic, minced
- 1 teaspoon dried oregano
- 1/2 teaspoon ground cumin
- Salt and pepper to taste
- 1 cup chicken or vegetable broth

Instructions:

Prepare the Poblano Peppers:
- Roast poblano peppers over an open flame, on a griddle, or under the broiler until the skin is charred.
- Place the roasted peppers in a plastic bag for a few minutes to steam, making it easier to peel the skin.
- Peel, seed, and stuff each poblano pepper with shredded queso fresco or Oaxaca cheese.

Batter for Chiles Rellenos:
- In a bowl, beat egg whites until stiff peaks form.
- In a separate bowl, whisk together egg yolks, flour, salt, and pepper until smooth.
- Gently fold the beaten egg whites into the egg yolk mixture.

Coat and Fry:
- Heat vegetable oil in a deep skillet or frying pan over medium-high heat.
- Dip each stuffed poblano pepper into the batter, ensuring it is well-coated.
- Fry the battered poblano peppers until golden brown on all sides. Place them on a paper towel to drain excess oil.

Prepare Tomato Sauce:
- In a saucepan, sauté chopped onions and minced garlic until softened.
- Add chopped tomatoes, dried oregano, ground cumin, salt, and pepper. Cook until the tomatoes are softened.
- Pour in chicken or vegetable broth and simmer until the sauce thickens.

Serve:
- Pour the tomato sauce over the fried chiles rellenos.
- Serve immediately, and enjoy these flavorful and cheesy stuffed poblano peppers!

Chiles Rellenos are often served with rice and beans or as a standalone dish with a side of Mexican crema and fresh salsa.

Agua Fresca de Sandía

Ingredients:

- 4 cups seedless watermelon, cubed
- 1-2 tablespoons sugar (adjust to taste)
- 1 tablespoon fresh lime juice
- 2 cups cold water
- Ice cubes
- Fresh mint leaves for garnish (optional)

Instructions:

Prepare the Watermelon:
- Remove the seeds and cut the watermelon into small cubes.

Blend Watermelon:
- In a blender, add the watermelon cubes and blend until smooth.

Strain (Optional):
- If desired, strain the watermelon puree using a fine-mesh sieve or cheesecloth to remove pulp. This step is optional, as some prefer the pulp for added texture.

Sweeten and Add Lime:
- Add sugar to the watermelon puree, starting with 1 tablespoon. Adjust the sweetness according to your taste preference.
- Add fresh lime juice to enhance the flavor.

Mix with Water:
- Transfer the watermelon mixture to a pitcher and add cold water. Stir well to combine.

Chill:
- Refrigerate the agua fresca for at least 1-2 hours to chill and allow the flavors to meld.

Serve:
- Pour the agua fresca over ice cubes in glasses.

Garnish (Optional):
- Garnish with fresh mint leaves for a refreshing touch.

Enjoy:
- Stir before serving and enjoy this delightful and hydrating Agua Fresca de Sandía, perfect for hot days or any time you want a refreshing beverage!

Feel free to adjust the sugar and lime juice to suit your taste preferences, and you can also get creative by adding a splash of sparkling water for some effervescence.

Carnitas

Ingredients:

For the Pork:

- 3-4 pounds pork shoulder or pork butt, cut into large chunks
- 1 orange, juiced
- 2 limes, juiced
- 1 cup chicken broth
- 1 onion, quartered
- 4 cloves garlic, smashed
- 2 bay leaves
- 1 teaspoon ground cumin
- 1 teaspoon dried oregano
- Salt and black pepper to taste

For Cooking:

- 2 tablespoons vegetable oil

Instructions:

Marinate the Pork:
- In a large bowl, combine pork chunks, orange juice, lime juice, chicken broth, quartered onion, smashed garlic, bay leaves, ground cumin, dried oregano, salt, and black pepper.
- Cover and refrigerate for at least 2 hours or overnight to allow the meat to marinate.

Cook the Pork:
- In a large Dutch oven or heavy-bottomed pot, heat vegetable oil over medium-high heat.
- Remove the pork from the marinade, allowing excess liquid to drain, and reserve the marinade for later.

Sear the Pork:
- Sear the pork chunks in batches until browned on all sides. This adds flavor to the carnitas.

Braise the Pork:
- Return all seared pork to the pot and pour in the reserved marinade. Add enough water to cover the meat.
- Bring the liquid to a boil, then reduce the heat to low, cover, and simmer for about 2-3 hours or until the pork is tender and easily shreds.

Shred and Crisp:
- Using two forks, shred the cooked pork in the pot. Continue cooking, uncovered, over medium heat until the liquid has evaporated, and the pork starts to crisp up. Stir occasionally.

Serve:
- Serve the carnitas in tacos, burritos, or as part of a bowl with rice and beans.

Optional: Crisp in Oven:
- For extra crispiness, you can transfer the shredded pork to a baking sheet and broil in the oven for a few minutes until the edges become golden and crispy.

Enjoy:
- Enjoy these flavorful carnitas with your favorite toppings, such as salsa, guacamole, cilantro, and lime wedges.

Salsa Verde Enchiladas

Ingredients:

For the Salsa Verde:

- 1 pound tomatillos, husked and rinsed
- 1-2 jalapeños (adjust to spice preference), stems removed
- 1 small onion, peeled and quartered
- 2 cloves garlic, peeled
- 1/2 cup fresh cilantro leaves
- Salt to taste

For the Enchiladas:

- 2 cups shredded cooked chicken (rotisserie chicken works well)
- 1 cup shredded Monterey Jack or Mexican blend cheese
- 1/2 cup sour cream
- 1/4 cup chopped fresh cilantro
- 1 teaspoon ground cumin
- Salt and black pepper to taste
- 8-10 small corn tortillas
- Vegetable oil for softening tortillas
- Additional cheese for topping (optional)

Instructions:

Prepare Salsa Verde:

Roast Tomatillos and Jalapeños:
- Preheat the broiler. Place tomatillos, jalapeños, quartered onion, and garlic on a baking sheet.
- Broil until the tomatillos and jalapeños have charred spots, turning them to char on all sides.

Blend Salsa Verde:
- In a blender or food processor, combine the roasted tomatillos, jalapeños, onion, garlic, and cilantro.

- Blend until smooth. Season with salt to taste.

Make Chicken Filling:

Mix Chicken Filling:
- In a bowl, combine shredded cooked chicken, shredded cheese, sour cream, chopped cilantro, ground cumin, salt, and black pepper. Mix well.

Assemble Enchiladas:

Preheat Oven:
- Preheat the oven to 375°F (190°C).

Warm Tortillas:
- In a skillet, heat a small amount of vegetable oil over medium heat. Briefly soften each corn tortilla in the oil to make them pliable.

Fill and Roll:
- Place a spoonful of the chicken filling in the center of each tortilla.
- Roll the tortillas and place them seam-side down in a baking dish.

Cover with Salsa Verde:
- Pour the salsa verde over the rolled enchiladas, ensuring they are well-coated.

Bake:
- If desired, sprinkle additional cheese on top.
- Bake in the preheated oven for about 20-25 minutes or until the enchiladas are heated through, and the cheese is melted and bubbly.

Serve:
- Garnish with additional cilantro, and serve the salsa verde enchiladas hot.

Enjoy:
- Enjoy these delicious and tangy Salsa Verde Enchiladas with your favorite toppings, such as avocado slices, chopped tomatoes, or a dollop of sour cream.

Cactus Salad (Ensalada de Nopales)

Ingredients:

- 2 medium-sized nopales (cactus paddles)
- 1 cup cherry tomatoes, halved
- 1/2 red onion, thinly sliced
- 1 jalapeño, seeds and membranes removed, finely chopped
- 1/2 cup fresh cilantro, chopped
- 1 avocado, diced
- 1 lime, juiced
- 2 tablespoons olive oil
- Salt and black pepper to taste
- Queso fresco (optional, for garnish)

Instructions:

Prepare Nopales:
- Using a sharp knife, carefully remove the thorns and eyes from the nopales.
- Rinse the nopales under cold water to remove any remaining thorns.
- Slice the nopales into thin strips.

Cook Nopales:
- In a pot of boiling salted water, add the nopales strips and cook for about 5-7 minutes or until tender.
- Drain and rinse the cooked nopales under cold water to cool them down.

Assemble Salad:
- In a large bowl, combine the cooked nopales, cherry tomatoes, thinly sliced red onion, chopped jalapeño, and diced avocado.

Make Dressing:
- In a small bowl, whisk together lime juice, olive oil, salt, and black pepper to create the dressing.

Combine and Toss:
- Pour the dressing over the salad ingredients.
- Gently toss the salad until well combined, ensuring the nopales are coated with the dressing.

Chill (Optional):

- Refrigerate the salad for about 30 minutes to let the flavors meld, or serve immediately.

Garnish (Optional):
- Garnish with crumbled queso fresco if desired.

Serve:
- Serve the Ensalada de Nopales as a refreshing side dish or as a topping for tacos.

Enjoy:
- Enjoy this nutritious and flavorful cactus salad with its unique combination of textures and tastes!

Birria Quesatacos

Ingredients:

For the Birria:

- 3 pounds beef chuck roast, cut into chunks
- 2 tablespoons vegetable oil
- 4 cups beef broth
- 4 dried guajillo chilies, stemmed and seeded
- 2 dried ancho chilies, stemmed and seeded
- 1 onion, chopped
- 4 cloves garlic, minced
- 1 tablespoon ground cumin
- 1 tablespoon dried oregano
- 1 teaspoon ground cinnamon
- Salt and black pepper to taste

For Assembling Quesatacos:

- Corn tortillas
- Shredded birria meat
- Shredded Oaxaca cheese or Monterey Jack cheese
- Chopped fresh cilantro
- Diced onion
- Lime wedges

Instructions:

Prepare the Birria:

Sear the Beef:
- In a large pot, heat vegetable oil over medium-high heat. Sear the beef chunks until browned on all sides.

Prepare the Chile Sauce:
- In a separate pan, toast dried guajillo and ancho chilies until fragrant. Remove from heat and soak them in hot water for about 15-20 minutes.

- In a blender, combine the soaked chilies, chopped onion, minced garlic, ground cumin, dried oregano, ground cinnamon, salt, and black pepper. Blend into a smooth sauce.

Braise the Beef:
- Pour the chili sauce over the seared beef.
- Add beef broth and bring the mixture to a boil. Reduce heat to low, cover, and simmer for 2-3 hours or until the beef is tender and shreds easily.

Shred the Meat:
- Once cooked, shred the birria meat with two forks.

Assemble Quesatacos:

Prepare Tortillas:
- Heat corn tortillas on a griddle or skillet until they are warm and pliable.

Add Cheese and Meat:
- Place a portion of shredded birria meat on each tortilla.
- Top with a generous amount of shredded Oaxaca or Monterey Jack cheese.

Fold and Cook:
- Fold the tortilla in half to create a quesadilla. Cook on the griddle until the cheese is melted, and the tortilla is crispy.

Serve:
- Serve the birria quesatacos hot, garnished with chopped fresh cilantro and diced onion.
- Serve with lime wedges on the side for squeezing over the top.

Enjoy:
- Enjoy these delicious and flavorful birria quesatacos, traditionally served with a side of consomé (broth) for dipping!

Mole Oaxaqueño

Ingredients:

- 4 dried ancho chilies, stemmed and seeded
- 4 dried guajillo chilies, stemmed and seeded
- 2 dried pasilla chilies, stemmed and seeded
- 1/2 cup sesame seeds
- 1/2 cup almonds
- 1/4 cup raisins
- 1/4 cup unsalted peanuts
- 1/4 cup pumpkin seeds (pepitas)
- 1/4 cup corn tortillas, torn into pieces
- 4 cloves garlic, peeled
- 1/2 large onion, chopped
- 1 teaspoon ground cinnamon
- 1/2 teaspoon ground cloves
- 1/2 teaspoon ground cumin
- 1/2 teaspoon dried oregano
- 3 tablespoons vegetable oil
- 4 cups chicken or vegetable broth
- 2 tablets Mexican chocolate (such as Abuelita or Ibarra)
- Salt to taste
- 1 to 1.5 pounds boneless, skinless chicken pieces (thighs or breasts)

Instructions:

Toast Chilies and Seeds:
- In a dry skillet over medium heat, toast the ancho, guajillo, and pasilla chilies until they become aromatic. Remove and set aside.
- Toast sesame seeds, almonds, raisins, peanuts, pumpkin seeds, and torn corn tortillas in the same skillet until golden. Be cautious not to burn them.

Soak Chilies:
- Place the toasted chilies in a bowl and cover them with hot water. Let them soak for about 20 minutes until softened.

Prepare Mole Base:

- In a blender, combine the soaked chilies (drained), toasted seeds and nuts, garlic, onion, cinnamon, cloves, cumin, and oregano. Blend into a smooth paste, adding water if needed.

Cook the Mole:
- In a large pot or Dutch oven, heat vegetable oil over medium heat. Add the mole paste and cook, stirring constantly, for about 10-15 minutes until it thickens and darkens in color.

Add Broth and Chocolate:
- Gradually add the chicken or vegetable broth to the mole, stirring to incorporate.
- Break the Mexican chocolate tablets into pieces and add them to the pot. Continue to cook until the chocolate is fully melted.

Season and Simmer:
- Season the mole with salt to taste. Add the chicken pieces to the pot.
- Bring the mole to a simmer, then reduce heat to low, cover, and cook for about 1.5 to 2 hours, or until the chicken is tender and cooked through.

Serve:
- Serve the Mole Oaxaqueño over rice or with warm tortillas. Garnish with sesame seeds if desired.

Enjoy:
- Enjoy the rich and complex flavors of Mole Oaxaqueño, a traditional Mexican dish known for its depth and richness!

Huitlacoche Quesadillas

Ingredients:

- 2 cups huitlacoche (canned or fresh)
- 1/2 onion, finely chopped
- 2 cloves garlic, minced
- 2 tablespoons vegetable oil
- Salt and black pepper to taste
- 8 small corn tortillas
- 2 cups Oaxaca cheese or Monterey Jack cheese, shredded
- Fresh cilantro, chopped (for garnish)
- Lime wedges (for serving)

Instructions:

Prepare Huitlacoche:
- If using fresh huitlacoche, clean it by wiping off any debris. If using canned huitlacoche, drain and rinse.

Sauté Huitlacoche Filling:
- In a skillet, heat vegetable oil over medium heat. Add chopped onion and minced garlic, sautéing until softened.

Add Huitlacoche:
- Add huitlacoche to the skillet and cook, stirring occasionally, until heated through. Season with salt and black pepper to taste.

Assemble Quesadillas:
- Warm the corn tortillas on a griddle or skillet. Place a portion of the huitlacoche mixture on one half of each tortilla.

Add Cheese:
- Sprinkle shredded Oaxaca or Monterey Jack cheese over the huitlacoche mixture.

Fold and Cook:
- Fold the tortillas in half, creating half-moon quesadillas. Cook on the griddle or skillet until the cheese is melted, and the tortillas are golden and crispy.

Repeat:
- Repeat the process for the remaining tortillas.

Serve:

- Serve the huitlacoche quesadillas hot.

Garnish:
- Garnish with chopped fresh cilantro and serve with lime wedges on the side.

Enjoy:
- Enjoy these unique and savory Huitlacoche Quesadillas as a delicious and distinctive Mexican dish!

Sopa de Lima

Ingredients:

For the Broth:

- 1 whole chicken, cut into pieces (or chicken pieces of your choice)
- 1 onion, peeled and halved
- 4 cloves garlic, peeled
- 2 carrots, chopped
- 2 celery stalks, chopped
- 1 bay leaf
- Salt and black pepper to taste
- Water (enough to cover the chicken)

For the Soup:

- 2 tablespoons vegetable oil
- 1 onion, finely chopped
- 2 cloves garlic, minced
- 2 tomatoes, diced
- 2 teaspoons ground cumin
- 1 teaspoon dried oregano
- 2 limes, juiced
- Zest of 1 lime
- 2 tablespoons achiote paste (optional, for color)
- Salt and black pepper to taste
- Corn tortilla strips (for garnish)
- Avocado slices (for garnish)
- Fresh cilantro, chopped (for garnish)

Instructions:

Prepare the Broth:

Boil Chicken:
- In a large pot, combine the chicken pieces, halved onion, garlic cloves, chopped carrots, chopped celery, bay leaf, salt, and black pepper.
- Cover with water and bring to a boil. Reduce heat and simmer for about 1.5 to 2 hours until the chicken is fully cooked and tender.

Strain Broth:
- Strain the broth, discarding the solids. Reserve the cooked chicken.

Make the Soup:

Sauté Aromatics:
- In a separate pot, heat vegetable oil over medium heat. Sauté finely chopped onion and minced garlic until softened.

Add Tomatoes and Spices:
- Add diced tomatoes, ground cumin, dried oregano, lime zest, and achiote paste (if using) to the pot. Cook until the tomatoes are softened.

Pour in Broth:
- Pour the strained chicken broth into the pot with the sautéed aromatics. Bring the mixture to a simmer.

Shred Chicken:
- While the soup is simmering, shred the reserved cooked chicken.

Season and Finish:
- Add the shredded chicken to the soup. Season with salt, black pepper, and lime juice. Adjust the seasoning to your taste.

Simmer:
- Let the soup simmer for an additional 10-15 minutes to allow the flavors to meld.

Serve:
- Ladle the Sopa de Lima into bowls. Garnish with corn tortilla strips, avocado slices, and chopped cilantro.

Enjoy:
- Enjoy this comforting and flavorful Sopa de Lima, a traditional Mexican soup with a zesty lime twist!

Cochinita Pibil Tamales

Ingredients:

- 2 pounds pork shoulder, cut into chunks
- 1 cup achiote paste
- 1/2 cup orange juice
- 1/4 cup white vinegar
- 4 cloves garlic, minced
- 1 teaspoon ground cumin
- 1 teaspoon dried oregano
- Salt and black pepper to taste
- Banana leaves, for wrapping

Instructions:

Marinate the Pork:
- In a blender, combine achiote paste, orange juice, white vinegar, minced garlic, ground cumin, dried oregano, salt, and black pepper. Blend into a smooth marinade.
- Coat the pork chunks with the marinade, ensuring they are well-covered. Let it marinate in the refrigerator for at least 4 hours, preferably overnight.

Prepare Banana Leaves:
- If using fresh banana leaves, briefly pass them over an open flame to make them pliable. Cut into large squares.

Assemble Cochinita Pibil Packets:
- Place a piece of marinated pork in the center of a banana leaf square. Fold the sides of the banana leaf over the pork to create a packet.

Steam Cochinita Pibil:
- Steam the cochinita pibil packets in a steamer for about 2 to 3 hours or until the pork is tender and fully cooked.

For the Tamale Dough:

Ingredients:

- 2 cups masa harina

- 1 cup chicken broth, warm
- 1/2 cup lard or vegetable shortening
- 1 teaspoon baking powder
- Salt to taste

Instructions:

Prepare Tamale Dough:
- In a large bowl, mix masa harina, warm chicken broth, lard or vegetable shortening, baking powder, and salt. Knead until you have a soft, pliable dough.

For Assembling Cochinita Pibil Tamales:

Ingredients:

- Cochinita pibil packets
- Tamale dough
- Banana leaves, cut into small squares for wrapping
- Kitchen twine

Instructions:

Assemble Tamales:
- Take a small portion of the tamale dough and spread it over the center of a banana leaf square.
- Place a cochinita pibil packet in the center and fold the banana leaf around it, securing with kitchen twine.

Steam Tamales:
- Steam the assembled tamales in a tamale steamer for about 1 to 1.5 hours or until the tamale dough is cooked and firm.

Serve:
- Serve the Cochinita Pibil Tamales hot, unwrapping them from the banana leaves before eating.

Enjoy:
- Enjoy these flavorful and aromatic Cochinita Pibil Tamales as a traditional Mexican dish with a unique twist!

Pollo con Mole Amarillo

Ingredients:

- 2 pounds chicken pieces (legs, thighs, or a whole chicken cut into pieces)
- 2 tablespoons vegetable oil
- 2 cups masa harina (corn dough)
- 4 cups chicken broth
- 4 dried guajillo chilies, stemmed and seeded
- 2 dried ancho chilies, stemmed and seeded
- 1 onion, chopped
- 4 cloves garlic, minced
- 1 teaspoon ground cumin
- 1/2 teaspoon ground cinnamon
- 1/2 teaspoon dried thyme
- 1/2 teaspoon dried marjoram
- Salt and black pepper to taste
- 1 tablespoon sugar (optional, to balance the flavors)
- Sesame seeds for garnish (optional)

Instructions:

Prepare the Mole Amarillo:

Toast Chilies:
- In a dry skillet over medium heat, toast the guajillo and ancho chilies until fragrant. Remove from heat and soak them in hot water for about 15-20 minutes.

Blend Chili Sauce:
- In a blender, combine the soaked chilies, chopped onion, minced garlic, ground cumin, ground cinnamon, dried thyme, dried marjoram, salt, and black pepper. Blend until smooth, adding water if needed.

Cook Mole Base:
- In a large pot, heat vegetable oil over medium heat. Pour in the chili sauce and cook, stirring constantly, for about 10-15 minutes until it thickens and darkens in color.

Add Chicken Broth:

- Gradually add the chicken broth to the pot, stirring to incorporate. Bring the mixture to a gentle simmer.

Prepare Corn Dough (Masa):
- In a separate bowl, mix masa harina with enough water to form a soft, pliable dough.

Thicken Mole:
- Take small portions of the masa dough and add them to the simmering mole, stirring continuously until the mole thickens to your desired consistency.

Season and Sweeten:
- Season the mole with salt and black pepper. Add sugar if needed to balance the flavors.

Cook Chicken:
- Season chicken pieces with salt and pepper. In a separate pan, brown the chicken pieces in vegetable oil over medium-high heat.

Combine Chicken and Mole:
- Add the browned chicken pieces to the pot of mole. Simmer for an additional 30-45 minutes or until the chicken is cooked through and the flavors meld.

Serve:
- Serve Pollo con Mole Amarillo over rice or with warm tortillas.

Garnish (Optional):
- Garnish with sesame seeds if desired.

Enjoy:
- Enjoy this delicious and flavorful Pollo con Mole Amarillo, a traditional Mexican dish with a yellow mole twist!

Tacos Dorados

Ingredients:

- 1 pound cooked and shredded chicken (seasoned with salt, pepper, cumin, and garlic powder)
- 12-15 small corn tortillas
- Vegetable oil (for frying)
- Toothpicks or taco holders
- Shredded lettuce
- Diced tomatoes
- Salsa or hot sauce
- Guacamole (optional)
- Sour cream (optional)
- Crumbled queso fresco or shredded cheese (optional)
- Chopped cilantro and sliced radishes for garnish

Instructions:

Prepare the Chicken Filling:
- Season shredded chicken with salt, pepper, cumin, and garlic powder. Ensure it's well-cooked and seasoned to your liking.

Assemble Tacos:
- Warm the corn tortillas in a dry skillet or on a griddle until they are pliable.
- Place a small amount of the seasoned shredded chicken in the center of each tortilla.
- Fold the tortillas in half, creating half-moon shapes, and secure them with toothpicks.

Heat Oil:
- In a deep skillet or frying pan, heat enough vegetable oil for shallow frying.

Fry Tacos:
- Carefully place the folded tacos into the hot oil, seam side down.
- Fry until the tacos are golden and crispy, turning them to ensure even cooking. This usually takes about 2-3 minutes per side.

Drain Excess Oil:
- Once the tacos are crispy and golden brown, use tongs to remove them from the oil and place them on a plate lined with paper towels to drain any excess oil.

Remove Toothpicks:
- Carefully remove the toothpicks from the tacos.

Serve:
- Serve Tacos Dorados on a plate lined with shredded lettuce.
- Top with diced tomatoes, salsa or hot sauce, guacamole (if using), sour cream (if using), and any other desired toppings.

Garnish:
- Garnish with crumbled queso fresco or shredded cheese, chopped cilantro, and sliced radishes.

Enjoy:
- Enjoy these delicious and crispy Tacos Dorados with your favorite toppings for a flavorful and satisfying meal!

Chile de Árbol Salsa

Ingredients:

- 20-25 dried chile de árbol peppers, stems removed
- 3 tomatoes, roasted
- 4 cloves garlic, peeled
- 1/2 onion, roughly chopped
- 2 tablespoons vegetable oil
- 1 teaspoon dried oregano
- 1 teaspoon salt, or to taste
- 1 cup water, or as needed

Instructions:

Prepare the Chiles:
- Remove the stems from the dried chile de árbol peppers. You can adjust the quantity based on your preferred spice level.

Roast Tomatoes:
- Roast the tomatoes over an open flame, on a hot griddle, or under the broiler until the skins are charred. This adds a smoky flavor to the salsa.

Soak Chiles:
- In a bowl, pour hot water over the dried chile de árbol peppers and let them soak for about 15-20 minutes to soften.

Blend Ingredients:
- In a blender, combine the soaked chiles, roasted tomatoes, peeled garlic cloves, and roughly chopped onion. Blend until you achieve a smooth consistency.

Sauté Salsa:
- In a saucepan, heat vegetable oil over medium heat. Pour the blended mixture into the pan.
- Add dried oregano and salt to the salsa. Stir well.
- Cook the salsa for about 10-15 minutes, stirring occasionally, until it thickens and the flavors meld.

Adjust Consistency:
- If the salsa is too thick, you can add water to reach your desired consistency. Adjust salt if needed.

Cool and Serve:

- Allow the salsa to cool before serving. This salsa is versatile and can be used as a condiment for tacos, grilled meats, or as a dipping sauce.

Store:
- Store any leftover salsa in an airtight container in the refrigerator for up to a week.

Enjoy:
- Enjoy the bold and spicy flavor of Chile de Árbol Salsa with your favorite dishes! Adjust the quantity of chiles to suit your spice preference.

Pulpo a la Gallega (Mexican-Spanish fusion)

Ingredients:

- 1 octopus, cleaned and tentacles separated
- 2 large potatoes, peeled and sliced
- 4 tablespoons olive oil
- 2 teaspoons sweet paprika
- 1 teaspoon smoked paprika
- 4 cloves garlic, minced
- Salt to taste
- Fresh parsley, chopped (for garnish)
- Lemon wedges (for serving)

Instructions:

Cook the Octopus:
- In a large pot of boiling salted water, immerse the octopus tentacles. Cook for about 45-60 minutes or until tender. You can check the tenderness by piercing the thickest part of the tentacle with a fork.
- Once cooked, remove the octopus from the pot and let it cool slightly.

Prepare Potatoes:
- In the same pot of boiling water, add the sliced potatoes. Cook until they are tender but not mushy. Drain and set aside.

Grill the Octopus:
- Preheat a grill or grill pan over medium-high heat.
- Brush the octopus tentacles with olive oil and sprinkle with salt. Grill for a few minutes on each side until they get a nice char.

Slice Octopus:
- Once grilled, slice the octopus into bite-sized pieces.

Prepare Paprika Oil:
- In a small pan, heat olive oil over medium heat. Add minced garlic and cook until it becomes fragrant but not browned.
- Stir in sweet paprika and smoked paprika. Cook for an additional minute, allowing the flavors to meld.

Assemble Pulpo a la Gallega:
- Arrange the sliced potatoes on a serving platter.
- Place the grilled octopus pieces on top of the potatoes.

- Drizzle the paprika oil mixture over the octopus and potatoes.

Garnish:
- Garnish with chopped fresh parsley.

Serve:
- Serve Pulpo a la Gallega warm, with lemon wedges on the side.

Enjoy:
- Enjoy this Mexican-Spanish fusion dish that combines the flavors of grilled octopus, seasoned potatoes, and a paprika-infused oil!

Pastel de Tres Leches

Ingredients:

For the Cake:

- 1 cup all-purpose flour
- 1 1/2 teaspoons baking powder
- 1/4 teaspoon salt
- 4 large eggs, separated
- 1 cup granulated sugar
- 1/3 cup whole milk
- 1 teaspoon vanilla extract

For the Three Milk Mixture:

- 1 can (14 ounces) sweetened condensed milk
- 1 can (12 ounces) evaporated milk
- 1 cup whole milk

For Whipped Cream Topping:

- 2 cups heavy cream
- 1/2 cup powdered sugar
- 1 teaspoon vanilla extract

Instructions:

Prepare the Cake:

> Preheat Oven:
> - Preheat your oven to 350°F (175°C). Grease and flour a 9x13-inch baking dish.
>
> Sift Dry Ingredients:
> - In a bowl, sift together the flour, baking powder, and salt.
>
> Beat Egg Yolks:
> - In a separate large bowl, beat the egg yolks with granulated sugar until light and fluffy. Add the milk and vanilla extract, mixing well.
>
> Combine Dry and Wet Ingredients:

- Gradually add the sifted dry ingredients to the egg yolk mixture, stirring until just combined.

Whip Egg Whites:
- In another bowl, whip the egg whites until stiff peaks form.

Fold Egg Whites:
- Gently fold the whipped egg whites into the cake batter until evenly incorporated.

Bake:
- Pour the batter into the prepared baking dish and bake for 25-30 minutes or until a toothpick inserted into the center comes out clean.

Cool:
- Allow the cake to cool completely in the baking dish.

Prepare the Three Milk Mixture:

Combine Milks:
- In a bowl, whisk together the sweetened condensed milk, evaporated milk, and whole milk.

Poke Holes:
- Once the cake is completely cooled, use a fork or skewer to poke holes all over the surface of the cake.

Pour Milk Mixture:
- Slowly pour the three milk mixture over the cake, making sure to cover the entire surface. Allow the cake to absorb the mixture.

Refrigerate:
- Cover the cake and refrigerate for at least 4 hours or preferably overnight to allow the flavors to meld.

Prepare Whipped Cream Topping:

Whip Cream:
- In a chilled bowl, whip the heavy cream, powdered sugar, and vanilla extract until stiff peaks form.

Spread on Cake:
- Once the cake has chilled, spread the whipped cream over the top.

Chill Again:
- Return the cake to the refrigerator and chill for an additional hour.

Serve:

- Slice and serve the deliciously moist and creamy Pastel de Tres Leches. Enjoy!

Note: You can garnish with a sprinkle of cinnamon or fresh fruit before serving if desired.

Pambazos

Ingredients:

For the Bread:

- 4 pambazo rolls (substitute: bolillos or soft sandwich rolls)
- 1 cup guajillo chile sauce (recipe below)

For the Filling:

- 1 pound chorizo, cooked and crumbled
- 4 medium potatoes, peeled, boiled, and mashed
- 1 cup refried beans
- 1 cup shredded lettuce
- 1 cup crumbled queso fresco or cotija cheese
- 1 cup Mexican crema or sour cream

For the Guajillo Chile Sauce:

- 6-8 dried guajillo chilies, stemmed and seeded
- 2 cloves garlic, minced
- 1/2 teaspoon ground cumin
- Salt to taste

Instructions:

Prepare the Guajillo Chile Sauce:

Soak Chilies:
- Place the dried guajillo chilies in a bowl and cover them with hot water. Let them soak for about 15-20 minutes until they are softened.

Blend Sauce:
- In a blender, combine the soaked guajillo chilies, minced garlic, ground cumin, and salt. Blend until you achieve a smooth sauce. If needed, add a bit of the soaking water.

Strain Sauce (Optional):

- For a smoother consistency, strain the guajillo sauce through a fine mesh strainer to remove any solids.

Prepare the Pambazos:

Prepare the Filling:
- In a bowl, mix the cooked and crumbled chorizo with the mashed potatoes.

Assemble the Pambazos:
- Cut the pambazo rolls in half and dip each half into the guajillo chile sauce, ensuring they are well-coated.
- Fill each roll with the chorizo and potato mixture.

Cook the Pambazos:
- Heat a griddle or large skillet over medium heat. Place the filled rolls on the griddle and cook until they are crispy and the filling is heated through.

Serve:
- Once cooked, top each pambazo with refried beans, shredded lettuce, crumbled queso fresco or cotija cheese, and a drizzle of Mexican crema or sour cream.

Enjoy:
- Serve the Pambazos hot and enjoy this delicious Mexican sandwich with a unique flavor!

Nopales and Egg Tacos

Ingredients:

- 1 cup fresh nopales (cactus paddles), cleaned and diced
- 4 large eggs
- 1 small onion, finely chopped
- 2 tomatoes, diced
- 2 cloves garlic, minced
- 1 jalapeño, seeds removed and finely chopped (optional, for heat)
- 1 tablespoon vegetable oil
- Salt and pepper to taste
- Corn tortillas (for serving)
- Fresh cilantro, chopped (for garnish)
- Queso fresco or cotija cheese, crumbled (for garnish)
- Lime wedges (for serving)

Instructions:

Prepare Nopales:
- Clean the nopales by removing thorns and spines. Dice the nopales into small pieces.

Cook Nopales:
- In a skillet, heat vegetable oil over medium heat. Add the chopped onion and garlic, sautéing until softened.
- Add the diced nopales to the skillet and cook until they are tender. This may take about 10-15 minutes. Season with salt and pepper.

Add Tomatoes and Jalapeño:
- Once the nopales are tender, add the diced tomatoes and chopped jalapeño (if using) to the skillet. Cook for an additional 5-7 minutes until the tomatoes are softened.

Scramble Eggs:
- Push the nopales and vegetables to the side of the skillet, creating space for the eggs. Crack the eggs into the skillet and scramble them until cooked through.

Combine and Season:
- Mix the scrambled eggs with the nopales and vegetables in the skillet. Season the mixture with salt and pepper to taste.

Warm Tortillas:

- In a separate pan, warm the corn tortillas.

Assemble Tacos:
- Spoon the nopales and egg mixture onto the warm tortillas.
- Garnish with chopped fresh cilantro and crumbled queso fresco or cotija cheese.

Serve:
- Serve the Nopales and Egg Tacos with lime wedges on the side.

Enjoy:
- Enjoy these flavorful and nutritious tacos for a delicious breakfast or anytime meal!

Chocolate Abuelita Pots de Crème

Ingredients:

- 4 ounces Chocolate Abuelita (Mexican chocolate), chopped
- 1 cup whole milk
- 1 cup heavy cream
- 4 large egg yolks
- 1/2 cup granulated sugar
- 1 teaspoon vanilla extract
- Pinch of salt
- Whipped cream (for garnish)
- Chocolate shavings or grated Chocolate Abuelita (for garnish)

Instructions:

Preheat Oven:
- Preheat your oven to 325°F (163°C). Place oven-safe ramekins or small jars in a baking dish.

Heat Milk and Cream:
- In a saucepan, heat the whole milk and heavy cream over medium heat until it just begins to simmer. Add the chopped Chocolate Abuelita to the hot milk-cream mixture.

Melt Chocolate Abuelita:
- Stir the mixture constantly until the Chocolate Abuelita is completely melted and the mixture is smooth. Remove it from the heat.

Whisk Egg Yolks:
- In a separate bowl, whisk together the egg yolks, granulated sugar, vanilla extract, and a pinch of salt until well combined.

Temper Eggs:
- Slowly pour the hot chocolate mixture into the egg mixture, whisking continuously to temper the eggs and avoid curdling.

Strain Mixture:
- Strain the combined mixture through a fine-mesh sieve into a bowl to ensure a smooth texture.

Fill Ramekins:
- Pour the custard mixture into the prepared ramekins or jars, dividing it evenly.

Create Water Bath:

- Pour hot water into the baking dish around the ramekins, creating a water bath. The water should come halfway up the sides of the ramekins.

Bake:
- Carefully transfer the baking dish to the preheated oven. Bake for about 30-35 minutes or until the edges are set but the centers are slightly jiggly.

Chill:
- Remove the pots de crème from the oven and let them cool to room temperature. Then, cover and refrigerate for at least 4 hours or overnight.

Garnish and Serve:
- Before serving, garnish each pot de crème with a dollop of whipped cream and chocolate shavings or grated Chocolate Abuelita.

Enjoy:
- Serve these delectable Chocolate Abuelita Pots de Crème chilled and savor the rich and indulgent flavors!

Salsa Macha

Ingredients:

- 1 cup dried chilies (such as arbol or cascabel)
- 4 cloves garlic, peeled
- 1/2 cup peanuts
- 1/4 cup sesame seeds
- 1/2 cup vegetable oil
- 1 teaspoon salt (adjust to taste)
- 1 teaspoon sugar (optional, to balance flavors)

Instructions:

Prepare Dried Chilies:
- Remove the stems from the dried chilies. If you want a milder salsa, you can deseed the chilies.

Toast Dried Chilies:
- In a dry skillet over medium heat, toast the dried chilies until they become fragrant. Be cautious not to burn them, as it can make the salsa bitter.

Toast Garlic and Peanuts:
- In the same skillet, add the peeled garlic cloves and peanuts. Toast until the garlic is golden and the peanuts are lightly browned.

Toast Sesame Seeds:
- Add the sesame seeds to the skillet and toast them until they are golden. Be attentive, as sesame seeds can quickly turn brown.

Blend Ingredients:
- In a blender or food processor, combine the toasted dried chilies, garlic, peanuts, and sesame seeds. Blend until you get a coarse mixture.

Heat Oil:
- In the same skillet, heat the vegetable oil over medium heat until hot.

Infuse Oil:
- Pour the blended mixture into the hot oil. Be careful, as it may sizzle. Stir continuously, infusing the oil with the flavors of the ingredients. Cook for about 5-7 minutes until the mixture darkens and becomes fragrant.

Season:
- Season the salsa with salt and sugar (if using). Adjust the seasoning according to your taste preferences.

Cool and Store:

- Allow the salsa macha to cool to room temperature. Once cooled, transfer it to a jar or airtight container.

Serve:
- Salsa Macha is incredibly versatile. Use it as a condiment for tacos, grilled meats, roasted vegetables, or as a dipping sauce. It adds a smoky and nutty flavor to your dishes.

Enjoy:
- Enjoy the rich and complex flavors of Salsa Macha with your favorite dishes!

Tacos Gobernador

Ingredients:

For the Shrimp Filling:

- 1 pound large shrimp, peeled and deveined
- 2 tablespoons olive oil
- 1 onion, finely chopped
- 2 cloves garlic, minced
- 1 cup diced tomatoes
- 1 jalapeño, finely chopped (seeds removed for less heat)
- Salt and pepper to taste
- 1/2 cup chopped fresh cilantro
- Juice of 1 lime

For the Queso Fundido:

- 1 cup shredded Oaxaca cheese or Monterey Jack cheese
- 1/2 cup diced bell peppers (assorted colors)
- 1/4 cup diced onions

For Assembling Tacos:

- 8 flour or corn tortillas
- Lime wedges for serving
- Additional fresh cilantro for garnish

Instructions:

Prepare the Shrimp Filling:

Sauté Shrimp:
- Heat olive oil in a skillet over medium heat. Add chopped onions and garlic, sauté until softened.
- Add shrimp to the skillet, cook until they turn pink and opaque.

Add Vegetables:
- Stir in diced tomatoes and jalapeño. Cook until the tomatoes release their juices and the mixture thickens slightly.

Season and Finish:

- Season the mixture with salt and pepper. Add chopped cilantro and lime juice. Stir to combine and cook for an additional minute. Remove from heat.

Prepare the Queso Fundido:

Melt Cheese:
- In a separate pan, melt the shredded cheese over medium heat until it becomes gooey and slightly golden.

Add Vegetables:
- Stir in diced bell peppers and onions. Cook until the vegetables are tender and the cheese is fully melted.

Assemble Tacos Gobernador:

Warm Tortillas:
- Heat the tortillas in a dry skillet or on a griddle until they are warm and pliable.

Assemble Tacos:
- Place a generous spoonful of the shrimp filling on each tortilla.
- Top the shrimp filling with a scoop of the queso fundido mixture.

Garnish:
- Garnish the tacos with additional fresh cilantro.

Serve:
- Serve the Tacos Gobernador warm with lime wedges on the side.

Enjoy:
- Enjoy these delicious and flavorful tacos that combine succulent shrimp with gooey cheese for a delightful dining experience!

Churros with Chocolate Dipping Sauce

Ingredients:

For the Churros:

- 1 cup water
- 1/2 cup unsalted butter
- 2 tablespoons granulated sugar
- 1/4 teaspoon salt
- 1 cup all-purpose flour
- 3 large eggs
- Vegetable oil (for frying)

For Coating:

- 1/2 cup granulated sugar
- 1 teaspoon ground cinnamon

For Chocolate Dipping Sauce:

- 1/2 cup heavy cream
- 4 ounces dark chocolate, chopped
- 1 tablespoon unsalted butter
- 1 tablespoon honey or corn syrup
- 1/2 teaspoon vanilla extract
- Pinch of salt

Instructions:

Prepare the Churro Dough:

    Combine Ingredients:
- In a saucepan, combine water, butter, sugar, and salt. Bring to a boil over medium-high heat.

    Add Flour:
- Remove the saucepan from heat and stir in the flour until a smooth dough forms.

    Add Eggs:

- Let the dough cool for a few minutes. Then, add the eggs one at a time, beating well after each addition. The dough should be smooth and sticky.

Transfer to Piping Bag:
- Transfer the churro dough to a piping bag fitted with a star tip.

Fry Churros:

Heat Oil:
- Heat vegetable oil in a deep fryer or a heavy-bottomed pot to 375°F (190°C).

Pipe Churros:
- Pipe 4-6 inch lengths of dough directly into the hot oil. Use scissors or a knife to cut the dough.

Fry until Golden:
- Fry the churros until they are golden brown and crispy, turning them to ensure even cooking. This usually takes about 3-4 minutes.

Drain and Coat:
- Remove the churros from the oil and drain them on paper towels. While still warm, roll them in a mixture of granulated sugar and ground cinnamon to coat evenly.

Prepare Chocolate Dipping Sauce:

Heat Cream:
- In a saucepan, heat the heavy cream until it just begins to simmer.

Melt Chocolate:
- Place the chopped dark chocolate in a heatproof bowl. Pour the hot cream over the chocolate and let it sit for a minute. Stir until the chocolate is completely melted and smooth.

Add Butter, Honey, Vanilla, and Salt:
- Stir in the butter, honey or corn syrup, vanilla extract, and a pinch of salt. Mix until well combined.

Serve:
- Serve the churros warm with the chocolate dipping sauce on the side.

Enjoy:
- Enjoy these homemade churros with a rich and decadent chocolate sauce!

Carne Asada

Ingredients:

- 2 pounds flank steak or skirt steak
- 1/4 cup orange juice
- 1/4 cup lime juice
- 4 cloves garlic, minced
- 1/4 cup chopped fresh cilantro
- 1 teaspoon ground cumin
- 1 teaspoon chili powder
- 1 teaspoon paprika
- 1/2 teaspoon dried oregano
- Salt and black pepper to taste
- 1/4 cup vegetable oil

Instructions:

Marinate the Steak:
- In a bowl, whisk together orange juice, lime juice, minced garlic, chopped cilantro, ground cumin, chili powder, paprika, dried oregano, salt, and black pepper.
- Place the flank steak or skirt steak in a large dish or resealable plastic bag. Pour the marinade over the steak, ensuring it's well-coated. Marinate in the refrigerator for at least 1 hour, or ideally, overnight for more flavor.

Preheat Grill:
- Preheat your grill or grill pan to medium-high heat.

Remove Steak from Marinade:
- Remove the steak from the marinade and let it come to room temperature for about 15-20 minutes.

Brush with Oil:
- Brush the steak with vegetable oil on both sides to prevent sticking to the grill.

Grill Steak:
- Grill the steak for 4-6 minutes per side, depending on your preferred level of doneness. Flank steak is usually cooked medium-rare to medium.

Rest the Steak:
- Once cooked to your liking, remove the steak from the grill and let it rest for a few minutes.

Slice and Serve:
- Slice the carne asada against the grain into thin strips.

Serve:
- Serve the carne asada on a platter or in tacos, burritos, or alongside your favorite Mexican dishes.

Optional Garnishes:
- Garnish with additional chopped cilantro, lime wedges, and serve with salsa, guacamole, or pico de gallo.

Enjoy:
- Enjoy the delicious and flavorful carne asada with your preferred sides for a fantastic Mexican-inspired meal!

Huaraches

Ingredients:

For the Dough:

- 2 cups masa harina (corn flour)
- 1 1/4 cups warm water
- 1/2 teaspoon salt

For the Toppings:

- 1 cup refried beans
- 1 pound cooked and seasoned protein (grilled steak, chorizo, or shredded chicken)
- 1 cup shredded lettuce
- 1 cup diced tomatoes
- 1 cup crumbled queso fresco or cotija cheese
- 1/2 cup chopped onions
- 1/4 cup chopped fresh cilantro
- Lime wedges for serving

Instructions:

Prepare the Dough:

> Mix Ingredients:
> - In a large bowl, combine masa harina, warm water, and salt. Mix until a soft, pliable dough forms.
>
> Knead Dough:
> - Knead the dough for a few minutes until it is smooth and elastic. If it's too dry, add a bit more water, one tablespoon at a time. If it's too wet, add more masa harina.
>
> Divide and Shape:
> - Divide the dough into portions and shape each into an oval or oblong shape, resembling a huarache sandal.
>
> Cook Dough:
> - Heat a griddle or non-stick skillet over medium heat. Cook each huarache for 3-4 minutes on each side or until cooked through and slightly golden.
>
> Assemble Huaraches:

- Spread a layer of refried beans on each huarache.
- Top with your choice of cooked protein (grilled steak, chorizo, or shredded chicken).
- Layer on shredded lettuce, diced tomatoes, crumbled queso fresco or cotija cheese, chopped onions, and fresh cilantro.

Serve:
- Serve the huaraches warm with lime wedges on the side.

Enjoy:
- Enjoy these flavorful and hearty huaraches as a delicious Mexican street food-inspired dish!

Guava Paletas

Ingredients:

- 2 cups guava pulp (fresh or canned)
- 1/2 cup water
- 1/4 cup honey or agave syrup (adjust to taste)
- 1 tablespoon fresh lime juice
- Optional: Chopped fresh mint leaves

Instructions:

Prepare Guava Pulp:
- If using fresh guavas, peel and remove the seeds. Blend the guava flesh in a blender until smooth. If using canned guava pulp, drain any excess liquid.

Combine Ingredients:
- In a bowl, combine the guava pulp, water, honey or agave syrup, and fresh lime juice. Mix well until the sweetener is fully dissolved.

Adjust Sweetness:
- Taste the mixture and adjust the sweetness by adding more honey or agave syrup if needed.

Optional: Add Mint (if desired):
- If you want to add a refreshing twist, stir in chopped fresh mint leaves into the guava mixture.

Pour into Molds:
- Pour the guava mixture into popsicle molds, leaving a little space at the top for expansion.

Insert Sticks:
- Insert popsicle sticks into the molds. If your molds come with a lid, cover them to keep the sticks in place.

Freeze:
- Place the popsicle molds in the freezer and freeze for at least 4-6 hours or until fully set.

Unmold and Serve:
- Once the guava paletas are frozen, run the molds under warm water for a few seconds to loosen the popsicles. Carefully remove them from the molds.

Enjoy:
- Serve these refreshing guava paletas on a hot day and enjoy the tropical flavors. They're a delightful and natural treat!

Poblano Cream Soup

Ingredients:

- 4 large poblano peppers, roasted, peeled, and chopped
- 2 tablespoons unsalted butter
- 1 onion, finely chopped
- 2 cloves garlic, minced
- 2 medium potatoes, peeled and diced
- 4 cups vegetable or chicken broth
- 1 teaspoon ground cumin
- 1 teaspoon ground coriander
- 1 teaspoon dried oregano
- Salt and black pepper to taste
- 1 cup heavy cream
- 1 cup milk
- 1 cup shredded Monterey Jack cheese
- Fresh cilantro, chopped (for garnish)
- Lime wedges (for serving)

Instructions:

Roast and Peel Poblanos:
- Roast the poblano peppers under a broiler or on an open flame until the skin is charred. Place them in a sealed plastic bag for 10 minutes, then peel, seed, and chop the roasted poblanos.

Sauté Aromatics:
- In a large pot, melt the butter over medium heat. Add the chopped onion and garlic, sautéing until softened.

Add Potatoes and Poblanos:
- Add the diced potatoes and chopped roasted poblanos to the pot. Cook for a few minutes, stirring occasionally.

Pour Broth:
- Pour in the vegetable or chicken broth, ensuring it covers the vegetables. Bring the mixture to a simmer and cook until the potatoes are tender.

Season:
- Add ground cumin, ground coriander, dried oregano, salt, and black pepper to the soup. Adjust the seasoning according to your taste.

Blend Soup:
- Using an immersion blender or transferring the soup to a blender in batches, blend until smooth. Be cautious as the soup will be hot.

Add Cream and Milk:
- Return the blended soup to the pot. Stir in the heavy cream and milk. Heat the soup until it's warmed through, but do not boil.

Melt Cheese:
- Add the shredded Monterey Jack cheese to the soup, stirring until the cheese is melted and the soup is creamy.

Serve:
- Ladle the poblano cream soup into bowls.

Garnish:
- Garnish each serving with chopped fresh cilantro.

Serve with Lime:
- Serve the poblano cream soup with lime wedges on the side.

Enjoy:
- Enjoy this comforting and flavorful Poblano Cream Soup as a delightful appetizer or a comforting main dish!

Chapulines Tostadas (grasshoppers)

Ingredients:

- 1 cup dried chapulines (grasshoppers)
- 1 tablespoon vegetable oil
- 1 clove garlic, minced
- 1/2 teaspoon chili powder (adjust to taste)
- Salt to taste
- Tostada shells
- Guacamole or avocado slices (for topping)
- Salsa (for topping)
- Fresh cilantro (for garnish)
- Lime wedges (for serving)

Instructions:

Prepare Chapulines:
- Rinse the dried chapulines in cold water to remove any debris. Pat them dry with a paper towel.

Sauté Chapulines:
- In a skillet, heat vegetable oil over medium heat. Add minced garlic and sauté until fragrant.
- Add the chapulines to the skillet. Sprinkle chili powder over them and toss to coat. Sauté for 3-5 minutes until the chapulines are heated through.

Season:
- Season the chapulines with salt to taste. Adjust the chili powder if you want more heat.

Prepare Tostadas:
- Heat the tostada shells according to the package instructions.

Assemble Tostadas:
- Spread a layer of guacamole or place avocado slices on each tostada shell.
- Spoon the sautéed chapulines over the guacamole.
- Top with your favorite salsa.

Garnish:
- Garnish the chapulines tostadas with fresh cilantro.

Serve:

- Serve the tostadas with lime wedges on the side.

Enjoy:
- Enjoy these unique and adventurous Chapulines Tostadas with a squeeze of lime for an extra burst of flavor!

Mezcal-Infused Chocolate Truffles

Ingredients:

- 8 ounces dark chocolate, finely chopped
- 1/2 cup heavy cream
- 2 tablespoons unsalted butter
- 2 tablespoons mezcal
- Cocoa powder, powdered sugar, or finely chopped nuts (for coating)

Instructions:

Chop Chocolate:
- Finely chop the dark chocolate and place it in a heatproof bowl.

Heat Cream and Butter:
- In a saucepan, heat the heavy cream and unsalted butter over medium heat until it just begins to simmer.

Pour over Chocolate:
- Pour the hot cream and butter mixture over the chopped chocolate. Let it sit for a minute to melt the chocolate.

Stir to Melt:
- Stir the chocolate and cream mixture until smooth and well combined.

Add Mezcal:
- Add the mezcal to the chocolate mixture and stir until fully incorporated.

Chill Mixture:
- Cover the bowl with plastic wrap and refrigerate the mixture for at least 3-4 hours or until it becomes firm enough to handle.

Shape Truffles:
- Once the chocolate mixture is chilled, use a spoon or melon baller to scoop out portions and roll them into small balls. Place the shaped truffles on a parchment-lined tray.

Coat Truffles:
- Roll each truffle in cocoa powder, powdered sugar, or finely chopped nuts to coat evenly. You can get creative with the coatings.

Chill Again:
- Place the coated truffles back in the refrigerator for another 30 minutes to set.

Serve:

- Once the truffles are set, arrange them on a serving platter.

Enjoy:
- Serve these indulgent Mezcal-Infused Chocolate Truffles and savor the delightful combination of rich chocolate and the smoky flavor of mezcal.

Queso Fundido with Chorizo

Ingredients:

- 1/2 pound (about 225g) Mexican chorizo, casing removed
- 1 tablespoon vegetable oil
- 1 small onion, finely chopped
- 1-2 jalapeño peppers, seeded and finely chopped (adjust to taste)
- 2 cloves garlic, minced
- 2 cups shredded Oaxaca cheese or Monterey Jack cheese
- 1 cup shredded Chihuahua cheese or asadero cheese
- 1/4 cup chopped fresh cilantro (for garnish, optional)
- Warm tortillas or tortilla chips (for serving)

Instructions:

Cook Chorizo:
- In a skillet over medium heat, cook the Mexican chorizo, breaking it apart with a spoon, until it's browned and fully cooked. Remove any excess grease.

Sauté Aromatics:
- In the same skillet, add vegetable oil. Sauté the finely chopped onion and jalapeño peppers until the onion is translucent.

Add Garlic:
- Add minced garlic to the skillet and cook for an additional 1-2 minutes until fragrant.

Combine Chorizo and Aromatics:
- Return the cooked chorizo to the skillet with the sautéed aromatics. Mix well to combine.

Melt Cheeses:
- Add the shredded Oaxaca or Monterey Jack cheese and the shredded Chihuahua or asadero cheese to the skillet. Stir continuously until the cheeses are fully melted and combined with the chorizo mixture.

Garnish:
- If desired, garnish the queso fundido with chopped fresh cilantro.

Serve:
- Serve the queso fundido with chorizo immediately while it's hot and gooey.

Accompaniments:

- Enjoy the queso fundido with warm tortillas or tortilla chips on the side.

Enjoy:
- Dig in and savor the rich and flavorful Queso Fundido with Chorizo! It makes for a delicious and satisfying appetizer or party snack.

Chile Ancho Rellenos de Picadillo

Ingredients:

For the Picadillo:

- 1 pound ground beef or pork
- 2 tablespoons vegetable oil
- 1 onion, finely chopped
- 2 cloves garlic, minced
- 1/2 cup raisins
- 1/2 cup chopped almonds or slivered almonds
- 1/2 cup diced potatoes
- 1/2 cup diced carrots
- 1/2 cup frozen peas
- 2 tomatoes, diced
- 1 teaspoon ground cumin
- 1 teaspoon ground cinnamon
- Salt and pepper to taste

For the Ancho Chiles:

- 6 dried ancho chiles, stemmed and seeded
- Hot water (for soaking)
- 1 cup queso fresco or shredded Monterey Jack cheese (for stuffing)

For the Batter:

- 3 large eggs, separated
- 1/4 cup all-purpose flour
- 1/4 teaspoon baking powder
- Pinch of salt

For Frying:

- Vegetable oil (for frying)

Instructions:

Prepare the Picadillo:

> Cook Meat:
> - In a large skillet, heat vegetable oil over medium heat. Add the ground beef or pork and cook until browned.
>
> Add Aromatics:
> - Add chopped onion and minced garlic to the skillet. Sauté until the onion is softened.
>
> Add Vegetables and Spices:
> - Stir in raisins, chopped almonds, diced potatoes, diced carrots, frozen peas, diced tomatoes, ground cumin, ground cinnamon, salt, and pepper. Cook until the vegetables are tender.
>
> Simmer:
> - Simmer the picadillo for 10-15 minutes to allow the flavors to meld. Adjust seasoning if needed. Remove from heat and let it cool.

Prepare the Ancho Chiles:

> Soak Chiles:
> - In a bowl, soak the dried ancho chiles in hot water for about 15-20 minutes until they become pliable.
>
> Stuff Chiles:
> - Carefully slit each ancho chile down one side, remove the seeds, and stuff them with the cooled picadillo. Insert a portion of queso fresco or shredded Monterey Jack cheese into each chile.

Prepare the Batter:

> Separate Eggs:
> - Separate the egg whites from the yolks.
>
> Whip Egg Whites:
> - In a clean, dry bowl, whip the egg whites until stiff peaks form.
>
> Mix Yolks and Dry Ingredients:
> - In a separate bowl, mix the egg yolks, flour, baking powder, and a pinch of salt until well combined.

Fold in Egg Whites:
- Gently fold the whipped egg whites into the egg yolk mixture until you get a smooth batter.

Fry the Chiles:

Heat Oil:
- In a large skillet or deep fryer, heat vegetable oil over medium-high heat.

Dip Chiles in Batter:
- Dip each stuffed ancho chile into the batter, ensuring it's fully coated.

Fry Until Golden:
- Carefully place the battered chiles in the hot oil and fry until golden brown on all sides.

Drain Excess Oil:
- Remove the chiles from the oil and place them on paper towels to drain any excess oil.

Serve:
- Serve the Chile Ancho Rellenos de Picadillo warm, garnished with additional queso fresco or shredded cheese if desired.

Enjoy:
- Enjoy these delicious and flavorful stuffed ancho chiles with picadillo!

Tequila-Lime Grilled Shrimp

Ingredients:

- 1 pound large shrimp, peeled and deveined
- 1/4 cup tequila
- 1/4 cup fresh lime juice
- 2 tablespoons olive oil
- 2 cloves garlic, minced
- 1 teaspoon ground cumin
- 1 teaspoon chili powder
- 1 teaspoon paprika
- Salt and black pepper to taste
- Wooden skewers, soaked in water for at least 30 minutes
- Lime wedges (for serving)
- Chopped fresh cilantro (for garnish)

Instructions:

Prepare Marinade:
- In a bowl, whisk together tequila, fresh lime juice, olive oil, minced garlic, ground cumin, chili powder, paprika, salt, and black pepper.

Marinate Shrimp:
- Place the peeled and deveined shrimp in a shallow dish or a resealable plastic bag. Pour the marinade over the shrimp, ensuring they are well-coated. Marinate in the refrigerator for at least 30 minutes, allowing the flavors to infuse.

Preheat Grill:
- Preheat your grill or grill pan over medium-high heat.

Thread Shrimp onto Skewers:
- Thread the marinated shrimp onto wooden skewers, piercing through both the tail and body of each shrimp.

Grill Shrimp:
- Grill the shrimp skewers for 2-3 minutes per side or until they are opaque and have grill marks. Be careful not to overcook, as shrimp cook quickly.

Baste with Marinade:
- While grilling, baste the shrimp with some of the reserved marinade to enhance the flavor.

Garnish and Serve:
- Once the shrimp are cooked, remove them from the grill. Garnish with chopped fresh cilantro and serve with lime wedges on the side.

Enjoy:
- Enjoy these Tequila-Lime Grilled Shrimp as a flavorful and zesty appetizer or as part of a delicious seafood meal!

Jicama and Mango Salad

Ingredients:

- 1 medium jicama, peeled and julienned
- 2 ripe mangos, peeled, pitted, and diced
- 1 cucumber, thinly sliced
- 1 red bell pepper, thinly sliced
- 1/2 red onion, thinly sliced
- 1/4 cup fresh cilantro, chopped
- Juice of 2 limes
- 2 tablespoons olive oil
- 1 teaspoon honey or agave syrup
- Salt and black pepper to taste
- Tajín or chili powder (optional, for garnish)

Instructions:

Prepare Ingredients:
- Peel and julienne the jicama. Dice the ripe mangos. Thinly slice the cucumber, red bell pepper, and red onion. Chop fresh cilantro.

Combine Vegetables and Fruits:
- In a large bowl, combine the jicama, diced mango, sliced cucumber, sliced red bell pepper, sliced red onion, and chopped cilantro.

Prepare Dressing:
- In a small bowl, whisk together the lime juice, olive oil, honey or agave syrup, salt, and black pepper to create the dressing.

Toss Salad:
- Pour the dressing over the jicama and mango mixture. Toss everything together until well-coated with the dressing.

Chill (Optional):
- If you prefer a chilled salad, cover the bowl and refrigerate for about 30 minutes before serving.

Garnish (Optional):
- Sprinkle Tajín or chili powder over the salad for an extra kick and flavor (optional).

Serve:
- Serve the Jicama and Mango Salad as a refreshing side dish or a light and crunchy snack.

Enjoy:
- Enjoy the vibrant combination of sweet mango, crunchy jicama, and fresh vegetables with a zesty lime dressing!

www.ingramcontent.com/pod-product-compliance
Lightning Source LLC
LaVergne TN
LVHW081558060526
838201LV00054B/1948